Love Letters & Children's Drawings

Norah Hanson was born in Hull in 1937. She spent much of the war in Beverley, before returning to Hull in 1943. She married Harry Hanson in 1957, graduated from Endsleigh Training College in 1978 and taught in secondary schools until her retirement in 1996. Widowed in 1994, she is nonetheless not short of company – she has six children, seventeen grandchildren and six great-grandchildren.

Her poetry has been published in numerous magazines and anthologies, and has had much competition success, including being shortlisted for the Bridport Prize and commended in the Yorkshire Open. *Love Letters & Children's Drawings* was Norah's first collection of poetry; a second volume, *Under a Holderness Sky*, was published in 2013.

Love Letters & Children's Drawings

NORAH HANSON

VALLEY

First published in 2011 by Valley Press
Woodend, The Crescent, Scarborough, YO11 2PW
www.valleypressuk.com

Reprinted in 2012, 2013 and 2014

ISBN: 978 0 9568904 6 7
Cat. no. VP0018

9 8 7 6 5 4 3

A CIP record for this book is
available from the British Library

Printed and bound in Great Britain by
Imprint Digital, Upton Pyne, Exeter

www.valleypressuk.com/authors/norahhanson

Contents

Acknowledgements

A number of these poems first appeared in the following publications: *Beneath the Surface* (Subtle Flame), *Dream Catcher, Eclipse, Harlequin, The Hull Connection* (Muesli Jellyfish), *In the Shadow of the Wolds* (Yorkshire Wolds Heritage Trust), *Iota, Partners, Patterns of Hope* (Bob Turner Memorial Trust / Valley Press).

'I Make Myself Blind' was longlisted for the Bridport Prize 2008, 'The Light of You' was shortlisted for the Bridport Prize 2009, 'Abandoned Fish Dock' was Commended in the Yorkshire Open Competition 2011.

'Abandoned Fish Dock' and 'Façade' were broadcast on BBC Radio Humberside in 2010.

For my children and grandchildren
and those who have journeyed before me

Springtime in Hull

A pair of swans on Barmston Drain
float under traffic on Beverley Road.
Washing dries in back gardens.
Easter eggs are on sale in 'Lidl',
bright trays of primula on
market stalls at '5 for £2'.

Crows' nests are refurbished in the
ancient trees of the old Convent.
A cat chases a squirrel in the ten-foot.
The quick mating of sparrows
on my garden fence. A teardrop
swell on up-thrusting daffodils.

Sunlight wakes me in my bed.

Abandoned Fish Dock

The largest fishing fleet in the world once sailed up the
Humber to the lock gates of this abandoned fish dock.
Handsome women with lined faces and chapped hands
gutted fish in open-sided sheds. The stench from the
fish meal factory would drift across the city on hot days.
Two-up and two-down houses tumbled from the quayside.

Decent washing was pegged across terraces, bloomers
dried indoors. Bookies' runners took bets in back alleys.
Lorries trundled in roads where children played.
Bobbers smuggled "fries" home under their jackets.
Corner shops gave tick; club cheques were paid weekly.
A good catch redeemed fur coats from pawn shops

to wear with black stockings and high heels when
wives linked arms with husbands for nights out in
Hessle Road pubs. As the men slept late into the day,
the women took money from their pockets, bought
talismans to guard against disaster and stayed home
when the trawlers sailed back to Arctic waters.

The abandoned Fish Dock; wind blowing off the Humber,
waste land, boarded buildings, 'Keep Out: Danger' signs
and fresh flowers by the tablet at the old Lock Gates
in memory of the men and boys who did not sail home.

Façade

The National Picture Theatre on Beverley Road was
bombed during the Second World War. It has been kept in
its derelict state as a reminder of the heavy bombardment
endured by the people of Hull. This poem was written after
reading the comments of a Councillor who referred to the
site as a 'badge of shame'.

Blitzed I stand, a silent unmoving relict in a world
of restless wanderers, animated computer-generated
war games, a Babel of words spinning in space.
Absence is an invisible buttress at my back
where couples once held hands and watched
their dreams come true on the flickering screen.

Children came later to harvest shrapnel in my rubble
and young girls with thin fingers pulled out the
delicate leaved plants to hold under their noses
and inhale the fragrance made from dust and death.

They used my broken bricks to build a stage
for little people, picked daisies and buttercups
thrusting for sunlight through my pebbled grit,
wore necklaces and wreaths of white and gold
as they danced and sang among the ruins of war.

I stand still in a road ripe for development.
My façade silent and fragile as a prayer,
an eyesore to those who forget, a monument to
those who died when bombs dropped on buildings
and machine guns strafed the streets of Hull.

My Granny Peed Like a Horse

Her home was a slum in Arthur's Terrace.
She drank a jug of Hull Brewery ale each night.
She'd send me to the 'open all hours' shop
to buy a penn'th of snuff and borrow a romance
from their lending library of tatty paperbacks.
We'd sit together on her horsehair sofa, holding
our books close to the light of the gas mantle,
which dimmed as the evening wore on.

She would lock the door of the outside toilet
when it wouldn't flush and the smell was bad.
I would crouch over the drain and marvel
at the hissing stream she ejected after lifting
her skirts to pee like a horse in the backyard.

She worked for a local tailor, turning collars,
fixing frayed turn-ups on trousers, buttonholing,
darning, patching; invisible mending she called it.
She stitched my school blouse, torn in a scuffle
with a bully who'd called her a 'dirty Irish peasant'.

In her thirties she lost her husband and three children.
Consumption it was – rampant in those days.
She'd prayed through the nights, 'Out of the depths
I cry to thee O Lord', and he hadn't listened.
Afterwards she hid in the cupboard when the priest called.

Her grandmother died in a ditch fleeing the potato famine.
Her grandfather was spat on arriving in Liverpool,
one of the diseased Irish bringing the plague with them.

I saw an asylum seeker today.
He was wiping spittle from his face.

Annie McGee

On Sundays, mam put a clean cloth
on the table, spread butter on thinly-
cut bread, sliced tomatoes, beetroot,
celery and the remains of the roast.
We ate jelly and custard for pudding.

Afterwards I played in the street
with hungry Annie McGee who
ate bread and dripping every day.
She asked about the taste of jelly
and custard. Was there any left?

Her house was dark and smelly.
Her mother stayed in bed all day.
Annie had no socks and spooned
sugar into her tea for breakfast.
She was always late for school.
I told her she was my best friend,
but I didn't tell my mother.

Annie McGee begged rotten fruit
from the greengrocer and once
snatched a banana, hid in the alley
and ate it whole, skin and innards.

Annie McGee always had nits, until
they shaved the hair off her head.
She swore at the boys who tried to
put their hands up her skirt.
Annie grew fat without food
and one day left the street.
I never saw her again.

Annie McGee was my best friend
but I didn't tell my mother.

Hell Fire

Mam would put the saccharin tablets
out of reach on the corner of the high
mantel shelf above the washing line
where our liberty bodices, woollies,
vests, socks and bloomers dried.
Rubber buttons on our liberty
bodices were squashed and misshapen
by the wooden rollers on the wringer.
Our woolly jumpers grew smaller
with each wash, until the sleeves
were up to our elbows and
the length above our rib cages.

My hand could fit in the gap in the
middle of the rollers on the wringer.
My brother threatened to turn the
handle and pull all of me through
if I didn't stop climbing onto the stool
and pinching the saccharin tablets.

He said he would make me flat like
my paper dolls, tear me into strips,
throw me onto the fire and laugh,
watching me curl up into grey ash.
Nobody would know where I'd gone
and he would never tell them.

I said that was a mortal sin and
he'd go to hell. Father O'Brien
wouldn't give him absolution
and he'd burn forever with the
dammed devils roasting him
on a spit, while I'd be an angel
in heaven. I might sometimes
fly over and feel sad for him,
but it would be his own fault.

Temple Street

Heatwave summer, when the swimming baths
closed and polio was epidemic.
'He'll never walk again,' we whispered,
sitting on the pavement, making hair slides
out of technicoloured plastic strips.
His sister bounced her ball against the wall
on the opposite pavement, where the houses
were cooler in the shadow of late afternoon.

Set apart she was, revered and feared.
Her brother a polio victim, paralysed
in a hospital bed and we unable to speak
to her for fear of contamination.

We waved grubby hands, but she tossed
her plaits and ignored us. We pretended
we didn't care, poked the leftover plastic
into the bubbling tar and hitched up our skirts
to tan our legs golden like Betty Grable.

The lads spread-eagled under the fierce sun,
skinny legs and bony ribcages blistering as
they willed their bodies into the brown muscled
perfection of the Cowboys and Indians they
cheered or booed at Saturday Matinees.

Our mothers stood in the doorways,
arms folded under bosoms, as they
waited for hospital visiting to finish
so they could nod sympathetically
to her mother, scurrying home
in her thin grey dress,
on the shadowy side of the street.

Divas in the Alley

A rusty bolt held the door shut.
Squared cuts of newspaper
sewn with string, hung
from the nail hammered
into the whitewashed wall.
Wind blew through the gap
under the door onto my feet.

I sang like Gracie Fields,
holding my top notes, until
a marble echo reverberated
round the walls. Song after
song, word perfect, tone perfect,
my hands holding the seat,
my legs swinging, my knickers
dangling on my ankles.

Down the alley, after her shift
in the factory, Doris sat in her
back yard sanctum to begin
her evening recital. Her voice
contralto, cello to my flute.

We sang in unison; arias from
the operas, love songs from
Hollywood musicals, family
favourites, Christmas carols.
Two caged street sparrows
escaping into dreams.

She Showed Me Her Dreams

On a winter day when frost crackled
static in the wireless, the window lost
light and dark slid through the glass
into my eyes, she poked the fire to
make the flames dance on the coals.

'Look,' she said, 'tell me what you see.'

I watched serpents glide from caverns,
their mouths wide. I saw forests fall
to ashes and children burning.
The devil glowered from the embers.
My face and knees prickled heat and
gravestone shivers chilled my spine.

She stood behind me against the cold.
'Look again,' she said.
'Can you see where the yellow is
growing golden? Can you see the
sun rising on the mountains?'

I looked and I saw, and I saw the
women striding into the dawn,
their gowns flickering red and green,
hurrying to meet the morning.

The Light of You

In the dreamtime before waking,
I lived again a winter afternoon
alone with you; the light fading
from the window, a coal fire,
the smell of baking bread,
the child I was listening as you
sang to music playing on the radio.

You twirled and clapped your hands.
I sat on the kitchen floor, flexing
my toes to the rhythm of your dance.
When the music stopped, my infant
voice called you to squat beside me.

Your smile crinkled lines round your eyes.
The light of you touched me.
I had no words to tell you this.

You stroked my hair, touched your lips
to my head. I butted into your warmth,
nuzzled into the smell of you.
You lifted me. Desire made me whimper
until my mouth filled with the flesh of you.
You wiped away my dribble.

Today you move your hand to the rhythm
of my voice singing the songs of your youth.
I stroke your hair, touch my lips to your head.
You whimper your need. I hold a drinking cup
to your mouth and wipe away your dribble.

Your smile crinkles lines round your eyes.
The light of you touches me.
I tell you this.

Where Dreams Made Blushes

Age lies sterile on white sheets,
gathering dust from sunbeams.
Shuffle of carpet slippers on
wipe-clean floors recedes,
leaving silence resounding
down empty corridors.
Parchment skin folds creases
where once dreams were writ.

A breeze lifts a net curtain.
A last faint breath escapes
through the open window,
is sucked into a sudden
rising wind, shaking
May blossom from trees,
tipping parasols on patios,
beneath a bruised sky.

Storm clouds whip a fury
chasing across the moors,
howling, pelting shards
to rain despair on sheep
huddled behind stone walls
where lovers once lay locked
in ecstasies and dreams made
blushes on eager lips.

Scattered

Handfuls of silk dust
drift through his fingers,
lift on the wind,
settle on boughs
bending over the river,
form globules for fish
to swallow and spit out.

That which you were is gone.
No flesh to rot beneath
a coffin lid sinking
under sodden clay,
no skeleton
template
under a
cross.

A talcum dusting inside an urn,
rinsed, poured out,
emptied,
gone.

On the Inside Looking Out

In night's silence the house sleeps,
breathing its own rhythm.
Beyond the window the garden
grows out of moon dust.
She watches spectral shadows,
children playing, puppy dogs
cocking legs at silver skirted
trees, ancients pottering;
hears after-echoes of laughter
held in swirls of mists.

Her palms press against the glass.
She passes through into moonlight.
Her ancient bones fold gently to
rest in the silence of the house.

Domestic Dilemmas

After futile attempts to fix the appliance,
I put on my glasses and squint at the small print
on the green page of the service manual.
I realise I am overdue for an eye test and seek
daylight to read the telephone number.

I join a queue listening to 'Air on the G String'.
Two cigarettes later, I am told my conversation
will be recorded for training purposes and Debbie
introduces herself and asks how can she help me?

Before I can explain my problem, she requires my name,
my postcode, my house number, the date of purchase,
the name of the store, the number on the invoice.

Because of past experience when I have tried the patience
of Debbie, Samantha, Kirstie, Linda and others, I have
the necessary information to hand and pace the kitchen
confidently as I speak into my cordless telephone.

Not to be outdone, Debbie asks me for the serial number.

I trip over the cat, my specs fall off, I drop the phone,
slam my funny bone on the back of a chair,
step heavily on my glasses, grind the lens to dust.
I pick up the phone, humbly ask where to locate
the serial number. She is no longer speaking to me.

Clear Your Clutter

My mother kept insurance, marriage and birth certificates
in a biscuit tin, to carry out should the house catch fire.
I am drowning in paper which I can't throw away in case
some official at some future date tells me I owe tax,
haven't paid a bill, did not read the small print as advised.

I save love letters, children's drawings, their school reports,
exercise books, certificates, fossils and rocks which fell
on my head when I opened the cupboard door in my son's
long vacated bedroom; birthday, anniversary, mother's day
cards, messages of condolence, ribbons, hair bobbles,
stub ends of pencils, used candles, a protractor, a T-square,
a compass, a metre-length wooden ruler, twelve one-foot
plastic rulers, knitting patterns, balls of wool, needles,
dry oil paints and brushes, children's annuals, my daughter's
Brownie uniform complete with Pixie symbol and badges.

The head of a silk daffodil sits in a wicker basket,
along with a rubber, two puncture repair kits,
a pencil sharpener without a blade, half a dozen
rubber bands, a squashed tube of super glue,
the end of a bicycle pump, two nails, one screw
and a brass cup hook speckled with green paint.

Zen and Feng Shui clear spaces, allow energy flow,
minimise clutter, achieve balance and harmony,
recommend that matter brought into the home
be equalled by matter leaving it.
I know this because I bought a book titled
'Clear Your Clutter' and I cleared my kitchen table,
saw the beauty of the wood grain, applied beeswax,
gazed in delight at the sheen, stepped back to admire,
stumbled on the piles of books stacked on the floor,
grabbed the curtains, brought down the rail,
smashed a vase, spilt my tea, bruised my bottom.

Too much energy released I reckon.

Don't Clear Your Clutter

Don't clear your clutter.
Leave surprises in bags
stored behind the settee.
Let apples grow wrinkles
sitting on worktops,
filling your kitchen
with cider smells.
Let the fire glow in winter.
Feed it logs to turn to ash
while the ancient dog
dream-twitches on the rug.
Pile up hats on your desk.
Fill your shelves with stones,
tins, books, potted mice.
Perch owls and blackbirds on
radiators, toucans, parrots
and seagulls on cupboard tops.
Dress the beautiful head of
the wooden maid in
sunglasses and wig
so she can smile at me.
Tumble photos of children
and babies on the piano top
next to opened glistening
chocolate wrappers,
offerings to the Gods.

Don't wind up the clock
on the mantel shelf.
Let it be forever the
midnight witching hour.
Light candles to glow on
heads of brass tigers
and leave your curtains
open to moonlight.
Let the paper birds in
their paper cages swing
in the chimney draught
and fish swim down walls.
Hang paintings, splashes
of your memories and dreams.

And make me tea when I come to visit.

Doors

There are forty-five doors in my house.
Layers of paint, fitted carpets and overflowing
cupboards prevent some doors from closing,
but on dark dismal nights when winds blow,
doors groan, creak open and slam shut.

Newly-fitted kitchen cabinet doors close easily,
but one brown knob regularly unscrews
and gets lost. I can open it by slipping a blade
into the side and levering. I have lots of bent knives.
My kitchen door has a sideways silver handle
which hooks onto clothes and handbags.
It likes scarves and is capable of strangulation.

My bi-locating vinegar jug plays hide and seek
behind closed cupboard doors.
I last saw it at Christmas.

The cupboard doors on the cabinet in my front room
have to remain closed, otherwise the drawer above
falls off its runners. I'm tempted to open them.
I think my vinegar jug could be hiding there.

A bed is jammed against the doors of a cupboard
in the main bedroom. Grown-up children who
complain about the mess their kids make
have left their own mess here; stacks of books,
Beano comics, smelly rucksacks, a broken guitar,
rocks, fossils, school exercise books, weightlifting
equipment and the side of a cardboard box with
A1 NORTH written in large black letters.

When I die, someone will open the doors in my house
and clear out all the clutter, some of which will finish
up in charity shops and be bought by rainy-day browsers.
My bi-locating vinegar jug could find a new hiding place.

The doors in my house may be taken off their hinges,
stripped and re-hung until fashion changes and paint
is re-applied. I would like to be able to float in the ether
on dark dismal windy nights when I would groan,
creak open doors and slam them shut before I leave.

Gremlins

Mischievous little buggers, they flash
around my home, plague my mind.
They have hidden my cordless phone.
It bleeps faintly somewhere in the kitchen
when I press the locate button on the base.
I've spent an hour trying to track it down.

I decide to concentrate on the day's business,
which requires a journey to my bedroom,
but they follow me and I arrive bewildered,
with absolutely no idea why I've come.
Down I go again, treading the frayed path
on my stair carpet, cursing my memory.

No sooner am I in the kitchen than I remember
I need the number I scribbled on the inside cover
of the book by my bed when the telephone woke
me up this morning. In charge again, I leave them
in the kitchen, climb the stairs and make the
necessary phone call from my bedroom.

*But down below, in the silent kitchen, they gently
nudge the plug sitting on the draining board,
which drops snugly into the plug hole, holding fast
the steady drip drip drip of water falling
into the sink from the leaking tap.*

Upstairs, I check my email, write a few letters,
change the sheets and clean the bathroom.
Two happy hours usefully spent.

And the water laps gently, slop slopping onto
the rim of the sink, drip dropping down
the cupboard door, seeping slowly, relentlessly
under the table, under the cooker and fridge.
They paddle gleefully in the pond of my kitchen floor.

Sensing their presence, my stomach knots in panic.
I race downstairs and stand defeated, ankle-deep in water.
The phone bleeps again, faintly, somewhere in the kitchen.

Squelching upstairs, I pick up the phone in my bedroom
and tell the salesman I don't need any double glazing.
He says he can't help me with my flood. I realise
I must pull out the plug, race downstairs, slither
in my wet slippers, wrench my ankle, hop to the sink,
lose my balance and splash down. The muffled bleep
of the phone sounds again in my floating kitchen.
I grab the fridge door, haul myself up, slip again,
struggle to stop the fridge falling on me as the door
swings open and bangs my head. Out plops my
phone into the water. It stops ringing then.

Concussed and bruised, they find me at six that night.
I lie in my hospital bed being questioned by a psychiatrist
who suggests a care home and medication. My son wonders
why he can't find my glasses and purse in my handbag.
I tell him to look in the fridge.

The Mugger

She walks the streets, hunting down her victims,
stops you with a friendly enquiry as to your health.
Once she has you captive, she'll tell you about her
bunions, arthritis, blood pressure, medication,
side effects, hip and knee operations, the mistakes
hospitals made when removing bits of her anatomy.
Bodily degeneration is her obsession.

For God's sake, don't give any hint that you are
less than fighting fit. Such information will
prompt the head-on-one-side gesture, the eyes
scrutinising your face, the hand pawing at
your shoulder, prophecies of doom bringing
you to despair, as you claw frantically for
the packet of Silk Cut in your handbag.

Imprisoned

Fettered as a fly caught in a spider's web,
fearful as a whimpering orphan,
I paint the walls cream, store pots and pans
behind new cupboard doors, spray the cooker
with anti-bacterial cleaner and sit alone,
bereft of disorder, listening to the hypnotic
tick-tock of the clock until it mutes the echoing
scream of the rape victim.

I remove a crumb from the pristine work surface
and sweep away the mess of binding relationships.
I fill in the grids on crossword puzzles, find logical
answers and hold at bay the unsolved struggles
of the dispossessed, the abused. I read a book
with a happy ending and blot out the press
pictures of crashed cars, dismembered bodies
and pavements spattered with blood.

Cocooned I am, as a fly in a spider's web.

Back to School in Beslan

September 2005

In Beslan, grandmothers are black-robed eagle guardians
of children starting a new term in a school gifted
from Moscow. They sit in classrooms, stand quietly
in playgrounds, hold the hands of their young ones,
walk them home past doorways where old men stare
into silent streets, hearing the echo of innocents at play.

Children draw pictures of men with staring eyes,
wolf teeth and snarling mouths, tear them into strips,
burn them to ashes, fill their homes with memories
of gunpowder and terror. The film crew focus on
the haunted faces of boys who vow to become soldiers
who can kill and avenge friends, teachers and fathers.
'Kids are already grown up,' one says.
'They understand everything.'

But one little girl smiles into the camera and speaks
of her dreams, of a time to come when blossoms will
flower in a spring orchard, growing from fields of blood
and the school will be a place where children
and teachers from Chechnya and Russia will come
to learn and play and grow together.

A Cold Coming

January 2008

They'd have a cold coming of it if they came today.
They'd find a bloody big wall around Bethlehem
and grim-faced young soldiers with Kalashnikovs,
demanding they show a pass, explain their purpose.

One star may shine the brightest but night vision
is blind in the radiance of sweeping search lights.
Angels may sing in the heavens, but ear drums, burst
in the thunder of explosives render shepherds deaf.

They have left their fields, their homes bulldozed,
their sheep scattered; they carry their slings into
David's town, pelt stones, scream defiance, make
weapons of their own bodies and die hating.

So what's changed since those dreamers journeyed
without a map, chasing a star across the heavens?
People still suffer under the brutality of the depraved,
the powerful, the greedy, the indifferent, the rich.

And hope limps bruised and battered, rising again
from the horror of holocausts, torture and betrayal.
Love refuses to die and there are those who believe
that somewhere, somehow, in the spaces between the
shifting matter, the flying bullets, the slaughter of
innocents, there is an energy which can conceive
a child of peace in the womb of a Maiden.

Daughter of the Troubles

Her mother and sister walked to Church
wearing black mantillas over their hair.
They walked with straight backs, clutching
their prayer books to their bosoms.

Her father led the telling of the Rosary
each Tuesday night after Benediction
at the Church of the Sacred Heart.
Himself and the priest retired to the pub
when the candles were snuffed to drink
whiskey and talk of the one true faith.

But she raced down the alley to meet
the lad with the brown eyes who marched
with the Protestants. He was an occasion
of sin and cost her dearly in confession.

And the candles and the sermons and the
click clack of the beads and the drunken
voices singing the rebel songs and the
car bombs and the kneecapping were not
enough to drown out the throb of her heart's
need for the lad with the brown eyes.

Transfiguration

12th March 2005

I sat alone at the front,
thinking myself a cut above,
listening to phone conversations
about bairns, price of fags, who's
sleeping with who, who's pregnant.

He boarded the bus, baseball cap
jammed on his head, leather jacket,
scruffy jeans, dirty trainers, his loud
voice asking how much for four stops.
He sat next to me.

'Bloody cold out there missus.'
I nodded. He caught my eye.
'Was in a café with me mum
yesterday, rained bloody
buckets on us as we left.'

I murmured something about
the severe weather forecast.

'Last week,' he said, 'I was in my
mate's flat. You could see this tree
through the window, snow on all its branches.
Bloody beautiful it was.
Bloody beautiful!'

As he pressed the bell and stood up,
the sun shone through the grimy windows
and he was bathed in light.
His eyes gleamed, his smile was radiant.
'Bloody beautiful,' he said.
'Bloody beautiful!'

Celtic Wedding

Rose petals scattered on grass.
In his green shirt, plaid cloak
and tartan kilt, the groom waits
on the cliff top. Guests gather,
the wind blows the rain out to sea.
The earth is the altar, the blue
white-tailed sky, the dome of heaven.
Dressed in flames she comes
to stand beside him.

No for better or worse in their vows,
but promises deep as oceans
and belief in a love stronger than death.

It was a glimpse of what will come
when church walls crumble,
and tabernacle doors fly open
and we can move beyond the laws
binding us in shame and guilt,
to risk and freedom, when creation
will tumble us into purifying fires,
and the heat of passion and the
breath of God will blow pure and clean.

Today there was a tissue-thin space
between heaven and earth
and I thought he walked again beside me.

I Make Myself Blind

When I could look on the beauty of him,
I made myself blind, to touch the bumps
and curves of his skull, drew my hands
across the width of his forehead, smoothed
the errant growth of his eyebrows, feather-
felt the swell of orbs leaping under silk skin,
flickered his lashes, pressed two fingers against
his eye sockets, sculpted the jut of his cheeks,
the length of his nose, the flare of his nostrils,
the fine groove above the twin arches of his mouth,
opened his lips, slid into moist softness, pushed
past ivory to rough tongue licking, dried my fingers
combing the bristle of his beard, kneaded the flat
of my thumbs against the strength of his jawbone,
pinched the folds and flexing of his ears, rested
two fingers on his temples and held his face
in the palms of my hands until I had taken the
carving of him into the marrow of myself and
imprinted his image behind my closed eyes.

Now, bereft of the sight of him, I make
myself blind to see and touch him again.

The White Wall

Flowers in my garden
exhale perfumes, swallowed
on an intake of breath.

Trowel in hand, I kneel by
stolen bricks painted white,
a crooked border for dreams
when money was food,
debt, cabbage seed and
I'd wanted more.

You'd made me fireworks,
blue, yellow, red, purple,
lavender, pink, marigold,
flashing on white alyssum.

I would have buried you there,
ground your bones to manure
and planted you hyacinths.
Instead, I breathe your sweat
made sweet from seeds you
scattered inside the white wall.

Shining through the Shadows

As you let go of thinning bones,
solidity and vitality, as your colour
faded, your skin became parchment
and only a shadow of you remained,
the spark within you burned brighter,
branding your glory on my vision.

I see you when I walk in forests.
I see you when friends celebrate.
You are there when we raise a glass.
I glimpse you in the smiles of our
children, I hear you in the echo
of their voices. You are in the spaces
between there and then and now,
shining through the shadows,
a translucent lingering glory.

I Thought It Was You

I thought it was you.
It could have been you;
the coat you wore,
the scarf loose on your neck,
the shadow at your back
thin on the shingle,
your hair loose curled on top,
trimmed close round your ears.

The face was nearly a likeness,
but lacking the lift of eyebrow
and height to the forehead.
He stood sideways to the waves,
feet together, hands in pockets,
back straight, self-contained
as a monolith on the beach.

If it had been you, I think
you would have faced the sea,
let the wind blow full in your face.
If it had been you, I think your
right arm would have been raised,
reaching back, your left leg
stepping forward, your back arched,
a stone in your hand to sling
flat popping over the waves.

If it had been you, I think
your mouth would have smiled
and I would have called your name,
if it had been you.

The Echo of Your Energy

I unlock the door ready for your coming,
but you ring the bell again and again,
summoning me to the crash of your arrival,
the unstoppable incoming tide of you.
You launch yourselves, cling like limpets,
your limbs fastened on my body,
your kisses wet on my face.

Sound surges, quietening the silence of
this house, and I am tumbled, tossed,
pulled in the gravity of your pulsing power.
All memories, all hopes become a now.
Alive and dead and here and there a now.
And I and you and them and us a now,
dancing in your faces, crying in your
tears, singing in your laughter until
I can hardly bear the wonder of you.

You leave and I listen to the echo of your
energy ringing in the silence of this
shipwrecked house as the clock ticks
and the emptied fridge hums.

Dandelion Dreaming

Dandelions sprang up by the water butt.
Beautiful, untamed as street urchins, they
flaunted green leaves and golden heads
like monstrance held aloft at Benediction.

A firework display in the tended flowerbeds
brought a rush of yellow, orange, pink, violet
and scarlet, jostling to drink the rain and bask
in sunlight before daffodils and bluebells
splayed satiated limbs, forget-me-nots
spilled seed and ground cover made lace.

I raked out the moist leavings of spring
and stood by the water butt as the breeze
breathed on haloed heads and dandelions
let go puffs of seed, fragile as lost dreams
drifting through the ages, until someone,
somewhere, will write a poem, think it new,
or maybe wonder where it came from.

A Breath of Silence

On walking the Wetlands in North Cave

I will stay out today,
leave behind me concrete
roads, crowded streets,
traffic and wailing sirens.

I will walk in Wetlands
where avocet feed,
tip-toeing in shallows.
I will watch the lapwing,
fringe-fingered, rising
on winds blowing over
diamonds glinting
on racing ripples.

I will tread ancient paths
where blackthorn blossoms,
greenfinch flit in sticky-
budded trees and birdsong
is caught in an echoing
past resounding on iron,
stone, gravel streams
and melting glaciers.

Beneath a blue expanse
of sky, where pillowed
clouds flicker shadows,
I will conjure wraiths
to walk with me, silent
creatures passing through
the veiled mists of time
into ages gone, to come,
where all is now held
in a breath of silence.

The Concrete Path

Three kites sail high above the Brigg,
bright coloured arcs in the blue sky.
The sea is gentle, lapping over the feet
of grandparents, letting children leap
over incoming waves, rocking swimmers.

A solo cornet player in the bandstand;
I hear again the tunes my father played
and seek refuge behind the hedge of
an enclosed garden where flower beds
blaze colour and silver lights the grass.

The wooden bench is named for a man
who loved this place. I breathe the air
he breathed and listen to your music.

A sparrow hops at my feet, pauses on
a tuft of infant grass sprouting in the
seam of the concrete path where
the dark grey meets the light grey
and yesterday touches today.

She Hums Quietly

She lies on her side picking daisies from the lawn.
At eleven years old, her body has curves.
Her hip rises from a slender waist.
Her legs are long, shapely and tanned.
Her brown hair glinting gold in the sun's heat.

'None of us would be here if it wasn't for you and
    granddad,'
she says conversationally.

The last to leave after the family gathering,
her mum is picking her up later.

I dig in the flower beds,
push pot plants into watered holes
and pause for a cigarette.

'True,' I say.

She hums quietly and I wish he was here
to see her growing beauty.
I remember hot afternoons when he dug
in the allotment which was then our garden,
planting cabbage, radish, onion, peas, carrot,
to feed hungry bellies.
Now I plant flowers and think of him.

She hums quietly, and I water the garden.